THE SCRUM MASTER: YOUR GUIDE TO PASS THE CERTIFICATION EXAM

BY

OUSSAMA KONTRA

Table of Contents

About the Author

Oussama Kontra, MBA, PSMI, ITIL V3, CSSGB™

Consultant – Business Analyst with more than 8 years of experience on delivering IT projects; Agile and ITSM projects.

Involved in the launching and realization of many large scaled projects, and having worked in several fields including industry, telecommunications, government and banking.

Holder of two master's degrees; one in information technology and an MBA. And many certifications. I had the opportunity to deliver courses and training in several areas of expertise including the Scrum.

About the certification

PSM (Professional Scrum Master) certification is issued by the Scrum Organization: Scrum.org.

CSM (Certified Scrum Master) certification is issued by the Scrum Alliance.

Both are recognized and reputed. And the preparation material is similar.

Regarding the Scrum.org PSM I certification, it is a 60-minute exam. 80 multiple choice questions. Completely and only in English.

The passing Score is 85%, which means that a minimum of 68 correct answers are required to pass the exam. In this book, you will find a concise and precise summary of all the elements you will need, to first, understand the Scrum and its implementation and pass your exam.

What is Agile?

IT project management is becoming a huge challenge in an ever-changing environment. Collecting and gathering all business and functional needs from the beginning of the project seems to be difficult. Complete project planning is a risky challenge for companies Nowadays.

The emergence of so-called "agile" approaches is essentially aimed at solving these challenges and reducing the risk of delivering a product that does not comply with customer requirements.

Agile approaches are increasingly replacing traditional project management methodologies like Waterfall methodology.

Waterfall, which might be more properly called the "traditional" approach is a linear approach to software development. In this methodology, the project is planned in its entirety, with well-documented specifications, and a clearly defined project plan in terms of financial and human resources ... Then starts the development phase: which include: the design, coding, testing, fixing ...

In an agile approach, the project is planned progressively, receiving continual feedback from customers to better understand their needs.

There are several agile approaches, but Scrum remains the most used agile approach.

Scrum: Agile framework

Scrum is not a methodology with specific processes and tools. It is one of the agile approaches that currently exist.

The agility of Scrum is often used when confronted with a field of activities where it is difficult to gather all the requirements upfront, or, when our customers keep changing their needs and all about what they want as a solution or service.

Scrum is an iterative and incremental framework for managing product development. It defines a flexible strategy where development team works as a unit to reach a common goal.

The Scrum approach allows you to have as many parts of the solution functional enough to be presented to customers and receive their feedback. This is called agility!

The delivery of product is iterative and incremental, which means the product will be delivered in working pieces, we keep adding features to it as we keep repeating the same development process.

We will see this development cycle in detail in the next pages.

THE SCRUM TEAM

The Scrum team:

There are three roles in the Scrum team, no more and no less. Adding other roles in the Scrum team is formally prohibited by the Scrum Organization.

The "Scrum team" refers to all project team members, and those are the three Scrum roles:

The Scrum Master   The Product Owner   The Development Team

Role #1: The Product Owner

Each project needs a business oriented person. In Scrum, this person is called "The product Owner". He/She is occupying this position full time in the project.

Product Owner's mission is to maximize the value of the product (the solution that we want to develop as we go along).

His/Her role is to maximize the work of the development team. Prioritizes and orders the needs expressed in "User Stories" according to their business value.

The Product Owner represents the Scrum team and presents the progress of the project to the various stakeholders including customers to allow maximum transparency (One of the values of Scrum).

Role #2: The Scrum Master

This is the person who best understands the different aspects of the Scrum. His/Her role is to coach the Scrum team to better adopt this approach, and ensure the smooth running by serving as a model and a leader.

It is a management position. The Scrum Master may be consulted by the Product Owner to help in making decisions.

Role #3: The Development Team

The development team refers to all the members that are responsible for delivering backlog items, and managing their own efforts.

This includes: architects, analysts, programmers, testers... All together are called "development team" by the "Scrum Organization".

There are no specific titles in a Scrum team (No Architect, no analyst, no programmer …). To enhance team spirit and collaboration.

The development team should be **Cross-Functional**: This means that they have all the expertise and competencies needed to get the job done without any help from outside the team. The team should also be **self-organized,** and that means: They must be able to self-manage and find their own way instead of receiving orders and being led by someone.

The development team is mostly effective when there are 3 to 9 members in each Scrum team.

SCRUM ARTIFACTS

· ·

The Artifacts

Scrum Artifacts are used to make Scrum implementation easier and more effective. They are designed to increase transparency of information related to the delivery of the project, and provide opportunities for inspection and adaptation.

Those are the most important artefacts of Scrum framework.

Artifact #1: The Product Backlog

It is an ordered list of everything that might be needed in the final product. In an agile approach, needs are added progressively in the Product Backlog after each meeting with customers to better understand their requirements.

The Product Backlog is never complete. We do not wait until the Product Backlog is complete to start delivering the items;

Needs are called "items". They are written as "User Stories" in a simple language as follows:

As a … I want to be able to …

This is a simple sentence, which tells a story of using the solution. Anyone should be able to understand it. In other words, the content should be non-technical. And each item should be independent (must not depend on any other item) otherwise agility will not be applied properly.

- **As an administrator, I want to receive an email notification when a new user is registered**

The Product Backlog is owned by the Product Owner. He/ She is responsible for the decisions concerning this artifact. His/Her is responsible for prioritizing items according to their business value (Product Owner can decide on how to calculate the items' business value, such as ROI: return on investment, etc. The Scrum does not recommend any particular tool).

The items in the Product Backlog are ordered in descending order. And every item could be broken down into "tasks" or "work" before being assigned.

ToDo List

ID	Story	Estimation	Priority
7	As an unauthorized User I want to create a new account	3	1
1	As an unauthorized User I want to login	1	2
10	As an authorized User I want to logout	1	3
9	Create script to purge database	1	4
2	As an authorized User I want to see the list of items so that I can select one	2	5
4	As an authorized User I want to add a new item so that it appears in the list	5	6
3	As an authorized User I want to delete the selected item	2	7
5	As an authorized User I want to edit the selected item	5	8
6	As an authorized User I want to set a reminder for a selected item so that I am reminded when item is due	8	9
8	As an administrator I want to see the list of accounts on login	2	10
Total		**30**	

Artifact #2: The Sprint Backlog

The Sprint Backlog is created during the Sprint Planning, it only contains the items that will be done in one Sprint (I will give you more details in next pages).

It contains items selected from the top of the Product Backlog based on their estimated work and the estimated capacity of the Development Team.

The Sprint Backlog is owned by the Development Team.

The selected items are detailed during Sprint Planning, and the Product Owner can provide explanations when needed.

Artifact #3: The Increment

It is a piece of working product. It is the result of completing a full Sprint.

Each Increment must be "Done", which means it should be potentially releasable/shippable and usable by the end users.

The Product Owner may or may not release a certain Increment, but it should be releasable nevertheless.

So, delivery is not necessarily required at the end of each Sprint, BUT the production of an increment potentially shippable and functional is required.

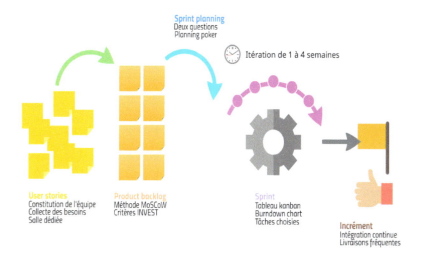

Sprint planning
Deux questions
Planning poker

Itération de 1 à 4 semaines

User stories
Constitution de l'équipe
Collecte des besoins
Salle dédiée

Product backlog
Méthode MoSCoW
Critères INVEST

Sprint
Tableau kanban
Burndown chart
Tâches choisies

Incrément
Intégration continue
Livraisons fréquentes

SCRUM EVENTS

Scrum Events

There are five events in a Scrum project: Sprint, Sprint Planning, Daily Scrum, Sprint Review, and Scrum Retrospective.

Before detailing each event, let's talk about the concept of "Time-Boxed Events".

"Time-box" is one of Scrum's most important concepts, allowing the development team to stay focused and guided by itself during the project development process. It is a **maximum time** that a Scrum event could reach, beyond which the event completes and they move directly to the next event.

EVENT #1: The Sprint

Each Scrum project delivers the product in several iterations, which are called Sprints. The Sprint is repeated cyclically, and contains the 4 other events.

In most companies, the Sprint is for a maximum duration of 2 to 4 weeks, usually 4 weeks. This duration is optimal so that the development team has enough time to complete a functional increment that is potentially releasable to the customer, without being too long for them to remain focused.

Each Sprint begins with a Sprint Planning, then a development phase where Daily Scrum's are scheduled daily, then a Sprint

Review and finally a Sprint Retrospective at the end of each Sprint.

The Sprint must be repeated as follows: Sprint number 2 must start IMMEDIATELY after the end of Sprint number 1. There is NOTHING happening between two Sprints.

The Sprint could be canceled by the Product Owner if the Sprint goal suddenly becomes OBSOLETE, due to a strategic change, such as the needs of the customer, the market or stakeholders.

A Complete Sprint

Sprint Planning	Daily Scrum's	Sprint Review	Sprint Retrospective

The Sprint repeats itself continuously until the delivery of the final product to the customer.

At the end of every Sprint, the Product Backlog is refined by the Product Owner and customers usually request changes during the Sprint Review.

EVENT #2: The Sprint Planning

Sprint Planning is the first event inside a Sprint. The Scrum Team picks the items they are going to deliver during the Sprint.

Instead of waiting to gather all the business and functional needs then start planning for the entire project.

The Development Team can, from the beginning of the project, go to the top of the Product Backlog and pick few items to start the first Sprint immediately.

The planning event is important and it is REQUIRED for each Sprint, it has a maximum duration of 8h for a Sprint of 4 weeks (4h maximum for a Sprint of 2 weeks).

During the planning event the Scrum Team collaborates on creating the Product Backlog. The development Team decides on the number of selected items, because they are self-organized and they know how much efforts they are able to put on every item. These items are usually simple and easy to understand, but the Product Owner could enlighten them in case of need.

The Scrum team agrees on a sprint goal.

During Sprint Planning, certain items can be broken down into multiple tasks to facilitate their achievement.

The Sprint Backlog with a sprint goal are the result of Sprint Planning.

Sprint planning = Creating Sprint Backlog
+ Sprint Goal AND estimate the work and
meaning for each item. Items are broken down
into tasks.

EVENT #3: Daily Scrum

After Sprint Planning, the development of the increment starts immediately. The Daily Scrum is held daily in 15 minutes by the development team - the Product Owner and the Scrum Master could attend Daily Scrum but they should not participate in the discussion. The objective of this event is that each member of the development team answers 3 questions and nothing more (lack of time!)

- What did I do yesterday?

- What am I going to do today?

- What obstacles are in the way?

Barriers are not discussed in the Daily Scrum, if one of the members would like to suggest solutions, he can do it after the end of the event.

The Daily Scrum is held in the same location and at the same time each day to avoid possible loss of time or confusion.

Daily Scrum is an opportunity for the team to align and synchronize in an optimal and efficient way.

The Scrum Master could help ensure the Daily Scrum runs smoothly, but he cannot ask questions or be a coordinator.

EVENT #4: The Sprint Review

Towards the end of the Sprint, when the increment is ready , let's call it "DONE", the Sprint Review is held for a maximum duration of 4 hours for Sprints of 4 weeks (2 hours for a Sprint of 2 weeks).

This is the opportunity for the Scrum team to present the increment to stakeholders and clients to receive proper Feedback.

The increment is presented ONLY when it is 100% complete and ready according to the "Definition of DONE".

The Product Owner then presents the project status using the Burndown chart of the project (an evolution chart).

Stakeholders are encouraged to express their demands and opinions, to help the Product Owner understand their needs.

The Product Backlog is reviewed by the Product Owner.

New items can be added, others can be deleted, and a new evaluation of the value and ranking of items can be done by the Product Owner.

EVENT #5: The Sprint Retrospective

The event has a maximum duration of 3h for a Sprint of 4 weeks, and proportionally shorter duration for a shorter Sprint.

This event is held just after the Sprint Review (at the end of the Sprint), also called "Lessons Learned" to discuss improving current processes, and looking for ways to improve the way we do things.

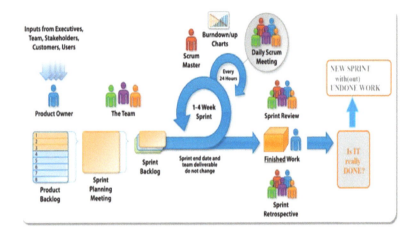

In Scrum framework, the entire Sprint cycle repeats itself until the product is up to the customer's expectations.

The Scrum approach enables effective agility through its simplicity and flexibility. It is simple to implement with no strict rules.

The Scrum Master must ensure that the Scrum Team has a good understanding of the Scrum cycle and can step in as needed to facilitate its application.

THIS IS HOW IT WORKS:

- Customers and stakeholders express their needs

- The product Owner creates a product backlog with the needs written as User stories

- The product Owner orders these items according to their Business Value

- The Sprint number 1 starts

- Sprint planning is the first Event

- Scrum team attends to the meeting and define a Goal for a Sprint

- The development team creates a Sprint Backlog: It's a certain number of items, they think they could complete in one sprint (Maximum 4 weeks)

- The work starts!

- Every day: 15 minutes of daily scrum is held. The development team answers 3 questions. The Scrum Master and The Product Owner could attend but could not Participate, which means, they don't answer the three questions

- Once the increment is ready and shippable, the Sprint review is held.

- The Product Owner and the development team will present the increment to the customers or stakeholders

- The Product Owner presents the status of project to them, demonstrating what is done and what remains as a work to complete the product.

- The customers will give their feedback, which helps the

Product Owner refine the Product backlog by adding or deleting some items and order them again according to their business value.

- Sprint Retrospective is the last Event, it allows to the team to think of ways to do things better.

- Once the 4 weeks are achieved, the Sprint is considered as complete

- The sprint is time-boxed and have a maximum duration.

- Sprint number 2 starts immediately after Sprint number 1.

- The same process is followed with the same events to complete another increment.

- The sprints are held one after the other until the final product is meeting customers' needs.

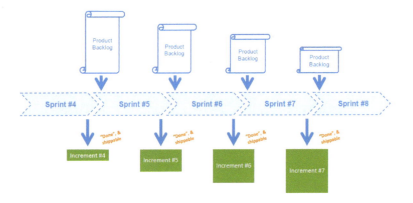

This illustrate how Scrum works. Product Backlog is getting smaller Sprint after Sprint.

Increment are getting bigger with more features and functionalities added by the end of each sprint.

Scrum: Other concepts

The " Definition of DONE "

The Scrum team must at the beginning of the project (Before Sprint 1) agree on things such as:

- The processes and tools used during the development of the solution.

- The non-functional features of the solution such as security, and performance...

- The criteria of quality and acceptance during the test phases.

This is a shared understanding of the DONE concept that relates to each increment made at the end of each Sprint. As we already agreed must be functional and potentially releasable to the customer.

This understanding is called "Definition of DONE", this concept is essential, because "items" do not cover all non-functional elements of the solution.

The Scrum Team, therefore, must share the DONE concept according to the agreed criteria that all together make a "Definition of DONE".

Monitoring Sprint/Project Progress:

Performance monitoring is essential for every project.

The Product Owner devotes a portion of his time to track and monitor the entire project using a "Product Burndown Chart" that illustrates what has been achieved and what remains to do to deliver a final product to the customer.

Time and Remaining Work are used to make the project status.

The Sprint Burndown chart is produced by the development team and it is used for monitoring the progress of every Sprint.

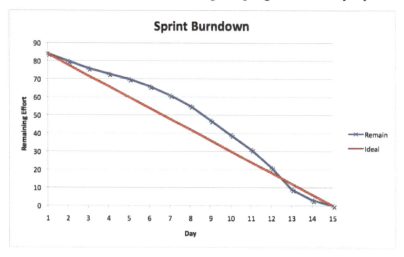

About Scrum:

Scrum is an approach (Framework) and not a methodology. This approach is based on an **Empirical Process** that is based on experience and observation to make decisions.

The Scrum empirical process is based on **3 essential pillars**:

Transparency: Scrum events allow transparency. The Daily Scrum is an opportunity to synchronize the progress of each member of the development team. The Sprint Review is an opportunity to communicate with all project stakeholders, and demonstrate team progress.

Inspection: The Sprint Review is the opportunity to present the increment and receive Feedback. The Product Owner is also consulted by the development team to validate the increment before the presentation

And **adaptation:** This is the pillar that best describes the Scrum. It is the opportunity to improve and change according to the result of inspection and transparency.

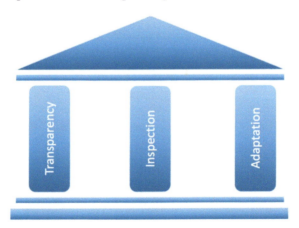

Other relevant information to pass the exam:

- The Product Owner has the power to make decisions concerning the Product Backlog.

- The development team has the final say on the Sprint Backlog

- The Product Owner is responsible for monitoring the entire project and presents it to stakeholders.

- The development team is responsible for monitoring Sprints and presenting Sprint status to the Product Owner as needed.

- The Product Owner is responsible for maximizing the value of the Product Backlog, adding new items continually as and when receiving feedback from customers.

- If the development team cannot complete the items promised for the Sprint, it is not a big deal. They should inform the Product Backlog for transparency.

- A Sprint could be canceled if the goal of the Sprint becomes obsolete or no longer meaningful. It is the Product Owner who makes the decision to cancel the Sprint.

- The Development Team is self-organized and does not need a team leader. All members are equal and independent. But even when reaching a maximum of maturity, a Scrum Master position is always needed in a Scrum Team.

- For the same project, there can be multiple Scrum teams. Only one Product Owner and one Product Backlog for a single project. On the other hand, there can be several Scrum Masters and several Development Teams for a single project.

- A development team has between 3 and 9 members.

- The Scrum Master's role is to facilitate the decisions of the development team by allowing them to remain self-organized and have their last word. Solve conflicts within the team, and ensure that the Scrum framework is understood by the entire team and properly applied.

- The Sprint Backlog is created by the development team at the Sprint Planning event (held at the beginning of EACH Sprint).

The Sprint Backlog can change during the sprint.

The Development Team can delete or add new items during the sprint. (from the SPRINT Backlog)

- The Scrum master and the Product Owner can attend the Daily Scrum but cannot participate and speak. Only the development team participates and answers the three questions during the daily Scrum Meeting.

- The Daily Scrum is always held at the same time and place, to reduce confusion and complexity.

Good luck!

- The exam consists of 80 questions mostly direct. However, it is necessary to pay attention to small details to avoid some basic errors.

- Differences of meaning.

- Example: Could, Should and Have to / Must

The Scrum Master could attend a daily scrum. (The Scrum Master can attend the Daily Scrum but He or She is not obliged).

The Scrum Master should attend a daily scrum. FALSE

The Scrum Master must attend a daily scrum. FALSE

- Example: The difference between the verbs "Attend" and "Participate"

The Scrum Master attends a daily scrum. TRUE

The Scrum Master participates in Daily Scrum. FALSE (Scrum Master and Product Owner can attend but not participate in Daily Scrum)

- The Project Manager or a Business Analyst are not roles of the Scrum team. There are ONLY 3 roles that are:

Scrum Master, Product Owner and Development Team

- For questions with multiple answers. The number of choices to be selected is always indicated in the question, so, pay attention to this detail to select exactly the number of good answers proposed.

GOOD LUCK!

www.ingramcontent.com/pod-product-compliance
Lightning Source LLC
Chambersburg PA
CBHW041155050326
40690CB00004B/574